# les Carnets de Dessins

Henri Scrépel

**BARRON'S, WOODBURY, NEW YORK**

*Printed in France*

Gustave Moreau
*Translated by Carol Martin-Sperry*
*Copyright © 1975 by Henri Scrépel, Paris.*

# Gustave Moreau's Universe

Sarane Alexandrian

# In the sphinx's lair

Gustave Moreau was the most mysterious creator of 19th century French painting' - to such an extent that his contemporaries never failed to compare him with his favorite creature, the sphinx. "He is the sphinx of painters," it was said in *le Musée Universel,* and this comparison was made many other times. Paul Leprieur, author of the first important article written about his work, wrote in *l'Artiste* of March 1889, "An isolated artist without precedents or successors, absolutely unique in style, Mr. Gustave Moreau presents himself to us as an enigma to be deciphered." He did not, however, accomplish anything particularly eccentric to merit such a strange reputation, other than to live alone in Paris in his house on the rue de la Rochefoucauld, without coveting honors, without taking pleasure in journeys and fashionable receptions, without even worrying about painting for all people. He admitted himself that he only wished to be

Narcissus.
Watercolor   53 x 61 cm.

Gustave Moreau Museum.

7

understood by an elite: *"The ambition of the artist is to become the friend and companion of people who are sensitive, delicate, great lovers, the only souls that one wishes to satisfy both in the present and in the future,"* he wrote in his unpublished diaries. Given certain concessions, he could have been the official painter of Napoleon III, who bought one of his paintings and invited him for a week to his court at Compiègne. But he preferred to shut himself in at his retreat, not take any holiday in the summer so as not to interrupt his work, yet disdaining more and more to exhibit his work, believing himself to be too far from perfection. One finds him disconcerting because one ignores the train of his thoughts, because his biography deals not with facts and deeds, but with all that came to pass within his brain throughout his life. Each of the figures that he painted is the result of a sum of dreams and meditations.

Contrary to Hippolyte Taine who at the same period maintained that art can be explained by race, environment, and climate, Gustave Moreau wanted his work to be judged independently from his person. He did not want any portrait of himself to show through; he gave no indication of his private life. He considered his painting to be a ministry, he forgot at all times the man that he was, so that he could become the great priest of the cult of Beauty, proud, uncompromising, obeying the most demanding scruples. Those who suspected him of expressing the impressions of hashish ("the imagination of an opium-smoker," said Henri Focillon of him), had no proof that like his homonym Moreau, a doctor of Tours, he ever experimented with the effects of hallucinogenic drugs. He apparently went through two or three spiritual crises, the motives of which we do not know. Only a few details are known about him: that he was for example very hot tempered or that he had a superb tenor's voice that earned him enthusiastic applause when he sang Mozart or Rossini in society. One could hear him singing from the street as he painted, and he boasted himself that he could interpret any of Wagner's operas from beginning to end. Apart from that, the strictest discretion comes into play when dealing with his loves and habits. His disciples who remain rigid with respect in his memory have kept the tradition of secrecy about him. The executor of his will, Henri Rupp, to whom we owe the arranging of his museum, refused to betray any confidence. Even to his intimate friends he remains a sphinx, asking questions about destiny, but whose destiny itself is a question.

If it were just a matter of honoring a painter of exceptional integrity, an author of visions that have an intense radiance, that would be reason enough to pay homage to Gustave Moreau. But his true interest is that of having been a precursor: he announced fauvism, expressionism, and surrealism; Henri Matisse and Georges Rouault were his respectful pupils, and Salvador Dali felt a fanatical admiration for him. There is not a painter right up to the movement of tachism who does not find a point of reference in him, for he signed studies that were simple notations of color done with a palette knife. One can see how wrong his contemporaries were who, like J-K Huysmans in *A Rebours*, considered him to be "without any possible descendants." It is essential to know his work in order to appreciate a whole current of ideas and feelings of which he is the best representative.

One tends to believe that impressionism was the only revolution in 19th century painting. Opposite the impressionists, who were fighting a tough battle with Manet, there was another innovating movement which ended in symbolism with Gustave Moreau as its leader. Edouard Manet and Gustave Moreau were the two antagonistic masters who were examples of the two main schools of painting at that time. Conscious of their opposing positions they fought while mutually respecting each other. Manet said, "I have a great sympathy for him, but he is following a bad route. People in society are in raptures over *Jacob and the Angel.* But Gustave Moreau, who is a believer, will have a bad influence over his time. He brings us to the incomprehensible, we who want everything to be understood." On his side Moreau said of Manet that he had no knowledge of composition and defined him as follows after his death: *"Manet had a very fine eye, but the total absence of style and matter in his work is detestable."* Manet and Moreau were the incarnations of the north and south poles of painting; one cannot abolish one or wish for him to have a different function, without compromising a vital balance. One wished to express modernity with scenes of daily life, the other wanted to express eternity with plastic poems; these two tendencies will always be found in painters in various different forms.

Joan of Arc.
Watercolor.

Gustave Moreau Museum.

10

Amateurs of Gustave Moreau's work made a distinction that was to become sharper and sharper between his watercolors and his paintings, not hesitating to prefer one to the other. When confronted with his vast mythological canvases, which were loaded with accessories, some showed a certain reticence, such as Edmond and Jules de Goncourt who wrote in their *Journal* in June 1876: "Gustave Moreau's talent is decidedly too much archaeology in a bowl of punch." But on May 15, 1881, having seen his watercolors, they went back on their judgment and said, "Curious, these watercolors of Gustave Moreau, watercolors of a goldsmith-poet that seem to be washed in the glow and patina of the treasures from *A Thousand and One Nights.*" The same sentiment is expressed in Odile Redon's *To Oneself,* where that original painter who is so well qualified to understand Moreau, declares: "The bright and lively watercolors that I shall call historic watercolors, develop fully and strongly, showing new charm in his somewhat rigid and cold manner. The *Phaeton* in particular is a work of great significance. Some memory of the beautiful outlines of Delacroix comes to mind in the presence of this brilliant page whose audacity and novelty of vision can be put on a par with the creations of that master." Only Redon, who was influenced by both Delacroix and Moreau, had the competence to make this comparison between them: "Delacroix has more abandon, more abundance; the power of his imagination takes him to the most varied subjects of history; above all he has more passion, and the supernatural light that falls on his entire work sets him apart and high up on the Olympus. But I can see in

Study for the Chimerae.
Watercolor . 22 x 33 cm.

Gustave Moreau Museum.

Moreau more excellence in the research, an exquisite and delicate penetration of his own consciousness as a painter. He knows what he wants and wants what he knows as a consummate and impeccable artist."

Today one is all the more inclined to turn to Gustave Moreau's watercolors in order to study his art in that one can be certain of not seeing his paintings as they appeared with their original brilliance to his contemporaries. Because of the continuous touching up that he did to them, the excess of highlights, of complicated mixtures, most of his paintings are obscured and do not allow one to discover the feeling of fireworks mentioned by all those who were the first to admire them. Toward the end of his life, Huysmans, not finding in his canvases the magnificence that he once enthused over, accused "the trickery of the paint merchants." He believed that the shades of the painter had become dull because he had bought low quality pigments. Such a thing can never occur in the watercolors which remain warm and vibrant, justifying all the praise that was given them, and even acquiring with time an extra velvety quality. Wandering through a selection of Gustave Moreau's watercolors – we will give proof of it here – is enough to see the moral problems, the aesthetic preoccupations, the themes, the tactile and visual sensitivity of this great initiator of modern art.

Ganymede.
Watercolor   24 x 35 cm.

Gustave Moreau Museum.

Gustave Moreau

# The years of initiation

From his childhood and youth Gustave Moreau was irresistibly drawn toward art, like a plant toward light. Born on April 6, 1826, in Paris he was the son of a liberal and cultivated architect who achieved a brilliant career under Louis Philippe, and who favored his son's vocation. In his old age the painter said to the young Matisse whose parents were less understanding, "There, everyone needs a father like mine, successful first of all, then very severe, inflexibly so for everything connected with work; an architect who lived among artists, who was consious of the great difficulty in judging a work of art, who never once imposed any of his ideas on me." After his studies at the College Rollin, Moreau entered the École des Beaux-Arts at the age of eighteen, to the studio of François Picot, which was considered to be a breeding ground for future prizes in Rome, and where many academic painters were formed, such

Ulysses and the Sirens.
Watercolor   42 x 30 cm.

Gustave Moreau Museum.

as Cabanel and Bouguereau.  He stayed six years, from 1844 to 1850, uneasy about the conventional attitudes that were taught him; he failed the Rome competition with his *Ulysses recognized by his servant.*  His admiration went out to Delacroix, the great rebel who was spurned by the members of the Institute; he made an effort to meet the master, but the latter, who did not take pupils, only gave him the vaguest advice.

Moreau then followed the example of Théodore Chassériau, a well-known young painter, who was attempting to reconcile classical drawing with color and romantic ardor. He had been a pupil of Ingres for a short time but had left him at the age of sixteen in order to continue his education alone. In 1848 Chassériau had just completed his allegorical decoration of the grand staircase at the Cour des Comptes (which was to burn down during the Commune); at the foot of the stairs grisaille panels symbolized Silence, Meditation, Study, Action, Idea; on the first floor Order and Force (paradoxically represented by a woman) preside over War, whose episodes of battles unfold along the staircase; on the top landing one can see the images of Peace and Commerce reconciling the people.  Moreau once took his father to visit the Cour des Comptes and said to him, "The author of these frescoes did not go through any studio in Paris. He worked simply by being inspired by the masters and antiquity."  The architect studied the paintings for some time and said to his son, "Well, do as he did.  You may now leave Mr. Picot."

Gustave Moreau rented a studio on the avenue Frochot, where Chassériau was already installed; now that they were neighbors he was able to visit him regularly

Pasiphae.
Watercolor   26 x 55 cm.

Gustave Moreau Museum.

The abduction of Deianira.
Watercolor    35 x 16 cm.

Gustave Moreau Museum.

The Return of the Prodigal Son.
Watercolor    12 x 29 cm.

Gustave Moreau Museum.

and study his methods.  Chassériau was a dandy with many feminine conquests, a retired cavalier, who painted wearing a white pique waistcoat and the clothes of high society.  But he was also a conscientious artist, remorselessly destroying a *Cleopatra* hired out to his admirers, that he was dissatisfied with.  A great personifier of woman, be it Venus, Andromeda, or St. Mary the Egyptian, he gave his most idealistic canvases a voluptuous and passionate feeling.  It is obvious that Moreau learned a lot from him; under his influence he interpreted his model more freely, he proceeded with great tones, and put into practice Chassériau's precept: "Do not fear great brilliance; nothing shines like nature, nothing is more radiant."

Moreau's relationship with Chassériau can be felt in his early works.  His *Pietà* with its life-size figures which he submitted to the Salon of 1852 was eclipsed by *The Sulamite* of the Salon of 1853 illustrating a passage from the *Song of Songs*.  These two paintings were bought by the State, as was *The Athenians delivered to the Minotaur* which he presented to the Exposition Universelle in 1855.  His beginnings were noted and encouraged, and already reflected his preoccupations, since it was at this time that he started *The Pretenders, Hercules and the daughters of Thestius,* to which he returned a long time later.

He was deeply affected in 1856 by the sudden death of Chassériau; in memory of his friend he painted *Death and the Young Man,* the first of his symbolist paintings. The handsome clean-shaven young man in his composition did not resemble Chassériau who had a black beard and a turned-up nose; behind him Death was represented in a most original way, by a young winged girl carrying a splendid sword. Not long after this event Moreau's personality changed; he became sad, refused to go to society meetings, read Pascal's *les Pensées* and *The Imitation of Jesus Christ;* he was turned in on himself and absorbed in his painting. His parents who were worried about his delight in being so morose encouraged him to make a journey to Italy; he left in October 1857 and stayed for two years.

He arrived in Rome convinced that he knew nothing despite his years of schooling and his success at the Salon, and that he should learn about the Renaissance. After getting his hand in by copying a fresco of the Sodoma at the Farnesina, he spent a month in the Sistine Chapel where he worked eight hours a day copying Michelangelo. Then he copied Jules Romains and Veronese at the Villa Borghese, then he saw a Raphael *Putto* at the Academy of St. Luke, "the most beautiful painting in Rome," and reproduced it by using a preparation of plaster on sized paper, imitating exactly the tones of the fresco. The tenants of the Villa Médicis, Elie Delaunay, Léon Bonnat, Henri Chapu who were joined by Degas, admired his ardor and his talent: "We were all mad about Moreau" said Bonnat later.

In the spring of 1858, without ceasing his activities as a copyist, Moreau made several visits to the Roman countryside and did sketches of nature. From that period there is a series of landscapes done in pen with sepia or watercolor highlights, revealing an unexpected aspect of his personality. It was always believed that Moreau was not interested in the open air, but those landscapes of Italy as well as the ones he did at Étampes in 1885 show that he was capable of being a landscape artist with an accurate eye and a precise hand.

Moreau went to Florence in June and from morning to night made copies at the Uffizi and Pitti palace; Degas came to join him, coming under his influence and took offence when Moreau left to greet his parents in Milan and accompany them to Venice. It was in the City of the Doges that Moreau found the masters that made the greatest impression on him: Mantegna, Bellini, Carpaccio (he copied his *The Return of the Ambassadors* and *St. George).* He returned to Florence, receiving urgent letters from Degas, then went to Rome before spending three months in Naples, which gave him the chance to copy in distemper the frescoes of Pompeii.

When he returned to Paris in October 1859, Moreau had acquired by his own means and with a discipline of steel, a profound knowledge of 15th-century painting. He had a good technique which he would use to express the views of his imagination. There remained, however, doubts and scruples which he confided to his best friend, Eugène Fromentin, who is considered today to be a writer but who at the time was a respected painter. He accepted the commission of a Way of the Cross for the church at Decazeville which was composed of fourteen unsigned paintings. He finished this series in 1862, the year that his father died, and it was believed that his desire for anonymity was the result of a religious vow. This theory is disputed. He was above all concerned with not putting his name to work which as we shall see did not correspond with the genre that he wished to create.

The Dead Lyres.
Watercolor   37 x 25 cm.

Gustave Moreau Museum.

# In the land of the chimerae

At the Salon of 1864 almost all the visitors agreed that one of the best paintings, if not the most important, was *Oedipus and the Sphinx* by Gustave Moreau. Although the painter was thirty-eight years old, he still appeared as a newcomer, for the few works he had shown ten years earlier had been forgotten; his arrival on the arts scene was interpreted as a brilliant debut and indeed his public career dates from that year. His chosen subject, which had often been exploited by the classical school, was treated by him in a modern pathetic way, giving it new life. The sphinx, a lioness with the head of a woman with unfolded wings and a string of red pearls girding its muscular loins, is digging its nails into Oedipus' chest; he is so contorted and despairing, so tormented that Théophile Gautier wrote that Moreau had painted a "Greek Hamlet." Most impressive of all is the fixed intense hypnotic look that is exchanged between Oedipus and the

The Magi.
Pastel    28 x 26 cm.

Gustave Moreau Museum.

Sphinx, like that of a trainer and his animal, each one trying to make the other back away by a menacing look; an interior violence emanates from these petrified beings, more vehement and fierce than that of people carrying out reckless deeds. Gustave Moreau used for the first time to the fullest extent two principles which were dear to him: the immobility of the figures and the wealth of accessories. There was nothing like the calm prescribed by Ingres who wanted figures to be painted at rest. In Moreau the figures are immobilized at the paroxysm of spiritual tension, at the moment when they touch the extreme point that separates balance from the fall, reason from madness. And the wealth, far from being a vain display of treasures, is the light of terrestial matter, in opposition or in answer to the light of the sky.

In the following years he elaborated this vein, and two camps were established around him, consisting of both admirers and critics. At the Salon of 1866 where he exhibited *Diomedes Devoured by his Horses* and *Young Thracian Girl Carrying the Head of Orpheus,* Castagnary the defender of realism sneered: "Your presence is requested at the funeral procession of Mr. G. Moreau, painter, two Salons old, who made an "Oedipus" but did not know to stop at the Sphinx: Orpheus and Diomedes will be the pall bearers." But Maxime du Camp replied: "Mr. Moreau is the master of the exhibition, for he has the best tendencies, the highest ideal, the greatest love for his art, the most radical disinterest in ephemeral triumphs, and the most obvious scorn for cliques." Faced with these reactions, Moreau spaced out more and more the presentation of his work; he took part in the Salons of 1869 and 1876, and in the Exposition Universelle of 1878; then after

Oedipus the Traveller.
Watercolor   35 x 25 cm.

Gustave Moreau Museum.

the Salon of 1880 he no longer showed any of his paintings in public.  He agreed to only two exhibitions of his watercolors.  Lovers of his work who came to see him were politely turned away; he behaved in this way from pride but also because he was very impressionable and he feared that their praise of their criticism would influence him.

Despite the diversity of his research, Moreau kept returning to the theme of Oedipus, with *The Sphinx's Cave, The Sphinx and the Corpse, The Conquering Sphinx.*  He felt that this was a dramatic situation that revealed the profound nature of man.  One could almost say from the emphasis he gives this myth that he had discovered the Oedipus complex before the psychoanalysts.  But he only retains the troubled relationship of man with the unknown, of the conscious with the unconscious.  The devouring Sphinx, whose terrible character he defines in many scenes, is the voice of the unconscious who, in the name of the obscure forces of the instinct, puts to man the insoluble questions about life, death, and the origins of the world.  It is the indefatigable questioner who engenders doubt, pessimism, and despair, who has to be overcome if one wants to go forward in whatever activity.

Moreau conceived of a rival to the sphinx who threatened to make man fall into an abyss: the Chimera, who sought to pull him up to the sky.  He painted a large canvas in 1868 showing a young girl with her arms around a winged horse with a man's head leaping off a mountain top; he leads one to see that the grasp will be loosened at any moment, and that

The Temptation of St. Anthony.
Watercolor    14 x 24 cm.

Gustave Moreau Museum.

30

the imprudent girl will fall into space: the symbol of the human soul clinging to a dream, being carried through the air by it, only to be shattered by deception. The theme of the Chimera is constant in Moreau, and leads him to represent all kinds of superior hybrids, centaurs, satyrs, androcephalic bulls, who are gods in disguise or the product of the union between gods and beasts. Their animalistic qualities assure the energy that they put at the service of their divine qualities. According to Moreau the mediators who carry the spirit from the real world to the land of Chimerae reconcile two extremes, the divine and the bestial. One is reminded of the dialogue between the Sphinx and the Chimera in *The Temptation of St. Anthony* by Flaubert (one of Moreau's favorite authors). In his own way the painter also illustrates the conflict between a fixed idea and a moving sensation.

His art, which attempted to make concrete his thoughts by means of symbols, was at the origin of symbolist poetry. Moreau's originality was that he had an influence on writers before he had any on painters. Novelists and poets were penetrated by his painting or cited him as the aesthetic model they were seeking for. J.-K. Huysmans is the best known but Jean Lorrain also worshipped Moreau. Henri de Regnier was inspired by him in his *Ancient and Romanesque Poems,* Bernard Lazare in his *Mirror of Legends;* Ernest Chesneau wrote his novel *The Chimera* after a painting of Moreau's, and many others from Francis Poictevin to Viélé-Griffin refered to him. The most turbulent of the symbolists appealed to Moreau, such as Joséphin Péladan who wanted him to join the catholic Rosicrucians and said of him when he refused: "I like him all the more because the bourgeois do not understand his canvases which are hermetic and painted for the initiated only." Robert de Montesquiou, a judge of elegance, was Moreau's faithful admirer and wrote his praises in *A Lapidary Painter,* where he recounted his first visit to the "little house" in the company of his cousin the Princess of Chimay and his daughter Elisabeth, the future countess of Greffulhe: "The little house was set back from the road, covered in parts in a rough orange paint against which the lilac wisteria blossoms made a pleasant contrast creating a somewhat Chinese-like harmony. In the entrance there stood a macaw with brilliant plumage – probably the prototype of many fabulous birds. Apart from this one sumptuous detail the inside of the house had a provincial coldness."

Because he was the favorite of the symbolist writers, Moreau was accused of being a "literary" painter. Such disparagement is not possible nowadays when one recognizes the impropriety of such a criticism. If among all the idealist painters of his time including Puvis de Chavannes and Carrière he is the only one to have the qualities of a master, it is indeed because of the texture of his forms which he fed with an inspired brush. Despite his vast culture ("Moreau knows everything," said Degas), he always lets himself be led by purely plastic motivation, "the love of the arabesque" and a taste for "beautiful color." For the rest he obeyed a feeling that he disclosed in his diaries: *one thing dominates me: the ardor and driving force toward abstraction. The expression of man's passions does without doubt greatly interest me, but I am led to make visible, if I may say so, the interior brilliance which has something divine about it.*

# The painter of the golden age

By his choice of subjects, his voluntarily sequestered life, what he showed of his philosophy in his work, Gustave Moreau was often taken to be a painter who was out of touch with his time, or even beyond it. It seemed as though he sought refuge in a far-off past in hatred of the present, that he sheltered behind mythology because he did not want to see the realities of life. Nothing could be further from the truth: if there is a certain disdain in him for the ugliness of the industrial society, one must admit that many of his contemporaries, the Parnassian poets, and the symbolists shared his point of view. Gustave Moreau is in many ways a man of his time but that did not mean that he should paint the Folies Bergères bar as did Manet or scenes observed at the racecourse and in the corridors of the Opéra. He was modern in a much more subtle way, by practicing an art that conformed with the movement of ideological renewal that occurred around him; he dealt with mythology by adding to it an imagination,

Job and the Angels.
Watercolor   30 x 23 cm.

Gustave Moreau Museum.

a wider view, an understanding of its sources which relate him to the ethnographs and philologists of the 19th century, not the neo-classicists who are attached to a conventional repertory.

Indeed for the cold followers of Louis David, painting mythological subjects was just a way of doing nudes, of grouping figures like antique bas-reliefs. For Moreau, it was a question of choosing a heroic myth, reflecting on the causes of its origins, dreaming about its consequences, expressing what is real about it not at any given period of time, but at all times. He was one of the rare artists who could call to mind the Graeco-Roman gods without ever making one think of a school exercice; and he was the only one to give us a glimpse of the orient beyond Greece. Yet it is in this that he is most definitely a man of his century, of that century wherein Max Muller created comparative mythology, and the scholars compared Greek civilization with the eastern civilizations. The Asiatic Society founded in 1882 by Silvestre de Sacy revealed Persian and Arabic texts; the correspondence of Victor Jacquemont published in 1824 gave its readers an enthusiasm for India, which he had visited in his capacity of "traveller for the natural history museum." Émile Burnouf translated the "Ramayana" from the Sanskrit, Ernest Renan began his work on Syrian and Hebrew epigraphy. Louis Menard revised in 1863 the notion of paganism in "of Hellenic polytheism." Michelet wrote "the Bible of humanity" (1864) to prove "the intimate relations of India, Persia, and Greece." Gustave Moreau was the painter of this erudite world who broadened the opinions that had been held on Antiquity; he owned in his library books of various human sciences (and even *Essays of Semantics* by Michel Bréal) that proved how attentive he was to the contemporary intellectual scope.

Autumn.
Watercolor   21 x 16 cm.

Gustave Moreau Museum.

However, although he was a fine connoisseur of new ideas about the myths, Moreau did not feel bound to make detailed archaeological reconstitutions of them. He criticized the Belgian painter Henri Leys whose speciality was representing scenes from the 16th century in a scrupulously accurate decor. He believed that painting should suggest, should awaken the desire for beauty and in order to do so should free itself from local circumstances. His method of working is syncretic and he sees no objection to mixing Brahman and Christian symbols, to joining together in architecture or in costume Greek, Indian, medieval, and romantic details. He has no desire to avoid anachronism. He does not hesitate to give Orpheus a halo, like a saint, if the image will gain in depth. He expresses in the same way a pagan subject, *Jason and Medea,* and a biblical subject, *Jacob and the Angel:* in both cases he portrays a young conqueror being led by a supernatural creature; in one case a magician, in the other an angel.

Gustave Moreau was not interested in just any myths. Most of the ones that he put into his work deal with the glorification of the Poet, showing either an episode of his passion, or a lyrical activity. The poet is the supernatural man, the true king of creation, who does not need to confront the Sphinx like Oedipus: his song delivers him. Moreau will portray Apollo, god of poetry, and his daughters, the nine Muses, sent out to enlighten the world. Then he exalts the first legendary poets, those who invented the essential forms of poetry: Hesiodus, the didactic rhapsodist, to whom tradition has attributed a theogony, a eulogy of agriculture, a calendar of happy and unhappy days; Tyrtaeus, inventor of

The Walk of the Muses.
Watercolor    29 x 22 cm.

Gustave Moreau Museum.

Gustave Moreau

the battle hymn, whose exhortations brought victory to the Lacedemonians; and above all Orpheus, sublimely inspired, versed in occult mysteries, who put nine strings on his lyre, and who moved to pity by his poems even the wild beasts and the infernal gods.

Orpheus is Gustave Moreau's favorite hero, he manifestly compares himself to him and wants to do paintings that are similar to the songs of Orpheus. He shows him in the different acts of the legend, but he also makes allusions to him in scenes where he does not appear, such as *The Journeying Poet, the Poet's complaints, The Poet and Nature, The Trials*. Moreau even approaches certain themes because they are related to the legend of Orpheus; for example the story of the Argonauts which was the subject of a vast canvas, was counted among the apocryphal works of Orpheus. Orpheus embarked on the ship Argo when Jason went in search of the golden fleece, and by singing he prevented the sailors listening to the sirens. When Moreau painted *The Sirens, The Poet and the Sirens,* he is referring to the journey of the Argonauts. He identifies with Orpheus to the extent that he deals with subjects in painting that are attributed to Orpheus in poetry.

The benefactors of humanity, the reckless adventurers of the ideal, Prometheus, Phaeron the son of the sun gravitate around the poet. The myth of Hercules, which greatly preoccupied Moreau, must be considered as a complement to the myth of Orpheus. Michelet said, "Hercules who one believes to be coarse, knew only the lyre. If he was the sometime rival of Apollo,

Study.
Watercolor    24 x 16 cm.

Gustave Moreau Museum.

40

Gustave Moreau

he is even more of a friend to him. He is the hero of the occident who persecutes the oriental Bacchus, feminine and furious." To Michelet Hercules is the Laborer, and Moreau makes a demi-god of him who, by purging the earth of its monsters, allows the poet to express himself in a pacified world. His different versions of *Hercules and the Lernean Hydra* (for which he did innumerable sketches of snakes in the *Jardin des Plantes), Hercules at lake Stymphalus* (where the birds have women's heads), *Hercules and the deed of Cerynia, Diomedes devoured by his horses,* show that the labors of Hercules serve the spirit by eliminating the agents of physical violence. Until then Hercules was depicted as a huge athlete, radiant with brute force; Moreau shows him to be a svelte and graceful young man whose power is almost spiritual, holding his club like a commanding officer's stick.

When Moreau composed *The Life of Humanity,* he unfolded in three triptychs images of the gold age, the silver age, and the iron age. It is obvious however, that he is above all a painter of the golden age, not the age that is completed, the lost Eden, but the one to come, the reward of man's virtues. He became the panegynist of youth and poetry so as to give us a presentiment, an anticipated vision. The heroes that he depicts are young and beautiful, so delicate that they are almost androgynous and their actions are idealized. He angrily reproached the impressionists for giving value to ugliness by painting common models and vulgar locations. He himself wanted to offer refined people magnificent spectacles, even if so much splendor did not correspond to reality, to indicate that the most noble human possibility is to reach for the impossible.

The Battle of the Centaurs.
Watercolor   15 x 28 cm.

Gustave Moreau Museum.

# The dream woman

One of the charms of Gustave Moreau's art is that he develops a poetic conception of woman which is translated into admirable hieratic figures. His melancholic heroines, haughty or swooning, at the confines of the legend, have made many a young man dream, such as Jean Lorrain who said, "Oh! He may boast of having forced the door to Mystery, he may revel in the glory of having disturbed his century, he has given a whole generation of artists, who are infatuated with mysticism and the beyond, a dangerous love for delicious dead girls from long ago, now resuscitated by him in the mirror of Time." *(Feelings and Memories,* 1895). The spectator asks himself what these dreamlike creatures correspond to, whether the painter raised them up to compensate for deceptive passionate experiences or whether he followed more general intentions. It is necessary to question his private life, to search for the reasons of these unreal apparitions.

Leda.
Watercolor   23 x 21 cm.

Gustave Moreau Museum.

Gustave Moreau had one great love during his life which led him to remain unmarried and which is at the origin of his feminine evocations: his mother. Pauline Moreau, who was a sensitive musician, had a very deep understanding with her only son, whose projects and hopes she wished to share; and he felt, as soon as she was widowed, that he should protect this fragile being who was agitated by the slightest emotion. They lived in proximity for twenty-two years in jealous intimacy like a couple who kept themselves to themselves. It was not that Moreau was not tempted to break his celibacy, to know other feelings than this filial love. Nobody can say who was the model for a portrait of a woman dressed in the style of the second Empire, hanging on the wall of his museum: it could be a lady from the court of Compiègne with whom he was in love. We know also that he fell for a young girl of fifteen who was his mother's companion during their stays at Honfleur. When she married he cried out in sorrow, *"She is marrying a man who will not understand her!":* he refused to greet her husband. Later the girl, by then Mme Sichel, recounted the anecdote to Edmond de Goncourt, saying that Moreau had at the time been most violent: "one day at Honfleur she arrived at the Moreau's just as his mother had broken something and he was in such a temper that she started to cry. But as soon as his anger had disappeared he asked forgiveness of his mother whom he adored, by being the tender son full of loving caresses." The affection between them was as strong as any passion, as was confirmed by Robert de

Leda.
Watercolor    39 x 24 cm.

Gustave Moreau Museum.

Montesquiou who said of the mother, "An ardent friendship united her with her son. Moreau tells me that once she got up in the middle of the night to throw some potion he wanted to take out of the window because she thought it was harmful."

The mother and son knew the tragedy of not being able to communicate: Pauline Moreau became totally deaf, saw no one, and relied on her only companion whose words she could not hear. In order to explain his work to her, Moreau wrote to her on little pieces of paper. One can imagine how sad it was for these two beings who were reduced to expressing themselves with signs when they had been used to such continual exchanges. In the house on the rue La Rochefoucauld he did not want any woman to usurp the place of his mother, nor to challenge her preeminence. When she died in 1884 he was upset for a long time and decided to give up the rare pleasures that he indulged in for the rest of his life. He justified himself to his pupil Georges Desvallières as follows: *You see, my dear boy, human nature is so weak that I am afraid of forgetting.* He had however started a liaison during his mother's lifetime which was a lasting one, but that he did not intend to regularize. Larroumet, who remembered that Moreau had forbidden speeches and wreaths at his funeral, added: "But he requested that the day he is lain to rest it should be in a anonymous tomb, covered in flowers, next to his mother. I was touched by this revelation of loyalty that was stronger than death."

Delilah.
Watercolor   25 x 18 cm.

Gustave Moreau Museum.

One understands Gustave Moreau's heroines better when one knows just how much he worshipped his mother. No real woman ever seemed to equal her, so he turned toward those whose beauty is sung in the myths. He could have married his mistress, or lived with her, but he did not so as not to wound his mother. He decided to allow in only the women of his dreams, and he wanted them to be extraordinary, so that the most sensitive soul could not be offended. And he felt no guilt in being in love with these imaginary women. Another of his pupils, Evenepoel, wrote: "Moreau is one of those men who consider themselves to be the lover of their works. He pays as much care and attention to them as he would to a person he loved." Indeed these works were inhabited by the only women he could love without remorse.

If one examines them closely, these figures seem to fall into three different types of women. One could say that he is trying to prove what is femininity and what it should be. The first type is Purity, or at least the beneficent woman who is the poet's accomplice. His well-known watercolor *Young Thracian Girl Carrying the Head of Orpheus* is very meaningful; Orpheus has been killed and dismembered by the furious Bacchantes, but a girl passing by has picked up his head and his lyre and carries them piously away. As Ragnar van Holten remarked so accurately, the young Thracian girl looks like the portraits of Pauline Moreau. The painter identifies his mother with her who takes the poet's remains away from his enemies. In *The Poet and the Saint,* the Pure girl takes roses from her dress and spreads them over her protégé; this watercolor which was copied from Chassériau's *Apollo and Daphné* is more mystical than religious. The Pure girl could be a real saint whose name is associated with a legend, but she could also be a virgin, a "lady with unicorn"; we know that the unicorn was the emblem of virginity in the Middle Ages.

His second type of woman is the Unchaste one, the great prostitute who insidiously captivates the senses and frees the evil forces in man. Moreau has an ambivalent feeling of fascination and horror for the Unchaste woman. No article of clothing or jewelry is too beautiful for her. He makes her deadly in her bearing, her apparel, her bodily form. He absolves her irresponsibility by showing that she proceeds like a sleepwalker, unaware of the harm she does, almost in sorrow and shame for what she is. It is Delilah, pensive, with candid eyes, turning away from the ruined Samson on his knees; it is Helen on the ramparts of Troy, holding a rose in her hand, indifferent to the corpses piled at her feet; it is Messalina or Pasiphae with their monstrous desires, Galatea exciting the cyclops Polyphemus to madness. It is above all Salome, whom Moreau repeated as a figure almost feverishly, Salome dancing gravely in front of Herod, Salome pacing up and down or lying like a panther, Salome the temptress, criminal, haunting, eternally dissatisfied.

From a Japanese Print.
Watercolor    23 x 18 cm.

Gustave Moreau Museum.

From a Japanese Print.
Watercolor    30 x 13 cm.

Gustave Moreau Museum.

Gustave Moreau — Exposition Japonais — au Palais de l'Industrie

Finally Moreau conceived of a third type of woman, the Initiated, who went beyond the Pure and the Unchaste because of her connections with the divine. Thus he painted Sappho as an Initiated woman, refusing to see her as a "damned woman" as Baudelaire did, but as the poet who invented the song of tears (mixolydian), the Sapphic rhythm, the bow for the lyre. Already Alcaeus sighed, "Black hair! Gentle smile!... Innocent Sappho!" And Michelet commented on this line, "This strong proud penetrating poet speaks a beautiful truth: genius is innocence." The fairy with the gryphon, the genie riding a dragon are also creatures who have acquired the mastery of fabulous beasts through initiation. But the supreme initiated woman for Moreau was Leda. The loves of Jupiter disguised as a swan with this nymph have provided the painters with an erotic theme for centuries; Moreau is the only one to treat it as a sacred act. He turns the myth of Leda into a pagan Immaculate Conception. The nymph receives a communication from the god, and her attitude is that of an officiating priestess, rather than that of a raped girl; she is fixed in ecstasy, opening to her being the secrets of the Cosmos. Her arm is raised, like the swan's neck, in an immobile dance which is the antithesis of Salome's sensual dance. Leda is everything that is best in a woman: a creature who attracts divine favor, and who obtains from this favor not terrestial advantages, but the power to give birth without losing her virginity.

From a Japanese Print.
Watercolor   30 x 25 cm.

Gustave Moreau Museum.

# The triumph of the fables

In 1880 at the age of fifty-four, Gustave Moreau undertook a singular enterprise, the illustration of La Fontaine's fables. His principal collector, Antony Roux commissioned this subject, which Moreau hesitated over at first; for he had a rule that he would never bend his art to a pre-defined programme, or an historical reality. He was at the time involved in important works and did not want to be distracted by a minor activity. Finally he had little affinity with La Fontaine, apart from his inclinations for dreams, his taste for solitude; he could not have felt any attraction for the poet's libertinage, or his laughing way of adapting the dramatic scenes, which he justified by saying in his preface "that one cannot brighten up the narration too much." La Fontaine's sobriety, which avoids descriptions, uses litotes and ellipses most cleverly and is quite opposed to the almost over-descriptive style of Gustave Moreau.

Illustration for a Fable of La Fontaine:

"The Oak and the Reed." Watercolor  31 x 22 cm.

Gustave Moreau Museum.

However, in order to please his friend, the painter chose some of the fables and began to look for their equivalent in watercolor; soon the general range of the collection, the possibilities that it offered him to express his own thoughts on the world were made apparent to him, and the project interested him deeply. He made many visits to the Jardin des Plantes to make sketches of all the animals - lions, monkeys, foxes, vultures, elephants - that he wanted to reproduce accurately.

In 1881 Gustave Moreau exhibited twenty-five watercolors from this suite at the Durand-Ruel gallery, along with the works of other artists, among them Gustave Doré and Élie Delaunay, who had also been asked to illustrate La Fontaine. The winner of this confrontation was Gustave Moreau, chosen unanimously by the press and the public. Even those critics who were usually hostile to his style succumbed to his charm. He alone had understood the deeper meaning of the fables, he alone gave one the desire to reread La Fontaine with a new understanding. Charles Blanc, a well-known aesthetician, wrote an enthusiastic review in *Le Temps:* "His watercolors on the Fables of La Fontaine make everything else look pale... one is taken to a region that is far from our minds, although the intensity of color brings it close to our gaze. Each of us is secretly reminded that painting here is the expression of supernatural things by the apparent imitation of the things of nature." His triumph was confirmed in 1886 when Gustave Moreau presented forty other watercolors inspired by La Fontaine at the Goupil gallery.

Illustration for a Fable
of La Fontaine:

"The Council Held by the Rats."
Watercolor    28 x 21 cm.

Gustave Moreau Museum.

These images, which were so fresh and delicate, in which decoration intermingled gracefully with the figures and backgrounds, were contrasted with his oil paintings, which some found to be solemn and stiff.

Carried away by his love of ancient architecture, damask linen, inlaid vessels, jewelry, the painter often gave his illustrations interiors and backgrounds from the Orient. *The Two Friends* with its line, "Two true friends lived in Monomotapa," gave him the chance to create a room in this ideal country, containing an idol, a column with a carved cornice, a giant candelabra, a panoply, a gazelle at the foot of a bed where there lay a naked slave, and the two friends dressed in sumptuous robes. *The Dream of an Inhabitant of Mogol* is a fairyland in which the person in jewelled mitre, covered in brocade, is lying on a balcony in front of a fantastic urban view while two spheres suspended in the air symbolize his dream and the hermit's dream. *The Peasant from the Danube* shows a fierce man leaning on a statue of the Roman shewolf in a square surrounded by porticoes. *The Rat and the Elephant* shows an elephant emerging from the jungle carrying a keeper and a kiosk with an Indian princess. In *The Cat Metamorphosed into a Young Girl,* a feline creature is standing in a room in a Persian palace lit by a gothic arched window. *The Vultures and the Pigeons* fight in the Nile valley above the head of the sphinx of Gizeh

Illustration for a Fable
of La Fontaine:
"The Animals Sick with the Plague."
Watercolor    30 x 21 cm.

Gustave Moreau Museum.

One can accept that Moreau unfolds panelling and monumental staircases, temples and antique columns, brilliant costumes for *The Two Adventurers and the Talisman, Jupiter and the Thunder, Love and Madness, An Animal on the Moon, The Matron of Ephesus, Democritus and the Abderites.* One admires him for showing in *The Lion in Love* a blonde woman with a red velvet hat and a dalmatic casually covering her nudity. But when he tackles the better-known fables of La Fontaine, the ones that seem to be inseparable from a 17th century French rustic decor, one is obviously disconcerted to see such wealth invade the countryside, contradicting the naivety of the anecdote, the tang of the soil that one expects to find.

At first glance one is led to believe that Moreau betrayed La Fontaine, or that he was very freely inspired by him, using his fables as pretexts; this was the belief of many commentators. Those who held this opinion supposed that the fabulist invented the content of his stories in verse, when in fact he always referred to older models. None of La Fontaine's fables belong to him as such, except for his inimitable style; he extracted the themes from his readings. It was once believed that the sources of La Fontaine were only Aesop, Phaednis, and the verses of the Middle Ages; we know today that he drew from all sides, even from oriental traditions. La Fontaine chose subjects for fables from the *Mythologica Aesopica* of Nevelet which assembles different Latin authors who imitated Aesop, such as Abstemius;

Illustration for a Fable
of La Fontaine:
"The Torrent and the River."
Watercolor    28 x 20 cm.

Gustave Moreau Museum.

he also borrowed from *the Book of lights, or the behavior of kings, composed by the sage Pilpay Indian* (Paris 1644), the first French version of the fabies of Bidpai. It is even thought that he wrote his fable "The Wishes" (Fables VI, Book VII) after a Hebrew work "The Parabolas of Sendabar on the Wiles of Women," which he would have read in the Latin translation by Gaulmin. So let no one say that Moreau turns La Fontaine away from his original meaning by placing visions of the orient round his fables; this orientalism of fantasy is in La Fontaine himself. *"The Cat, the Weasel and the Little Rabbit"* is a fable of Indian origin; *"The Milkmaid and the Jug of Milk"* is a story found in two sanskrit collections, the *"Pantshatantra"* and the *"Hitopadesa,"* as well as in Bidpai. By giving these French poems an illustration that reminds one of India and Persia, Moreau is carrying out an extremely accurate interpretation of his subject: he sets free the universal by means of the particular.

Let us take for example *"the Town Rat and the Country Rat";* before La Fontaine this fable had been treated successively by Aesop, Babrius, Aphtonius, Horace, Romulus, Corrozet, Eustache the Noble; and after him poets of the 18th century such as Andrieux and Collin d'Harleville had attempted to treat it in a new light. So there was no need for Gustave Moreau to paint the subject as though it were the property of a French poet from the century of Louis XIV; he places the two rats on a table richly decorated with flagons, goblets, ewers, a bowl carrying a pyramid of fruit.

Illustration for a Fable
of La Fontaine:

"The Two Ducks and the Tortoise."
Watercolor   28 x 18 cm.

Gustave Moreau Museum.

This composite decor with its pieces of furniture from different centuries, including the chair and the mirror, shows that the scene it contains is of all time.

For the fables that we all know by heart, he looks for surprise in the contrast, or in the dramatization itself. To illustrate *"The Cricket and the Ant,"* he depicts the cricket as a sprightly young musician with a lute slung across her back, passing in front of the home of a rough little worker, the ant. In *The oak and the Reed* where the countryside shakes in the storm, *The Fox and the Crow, The Frogs seeking a king, The Fox and the Grapes* and in all the confrontations of animals that he imagines under a menacing sky, in the bloodred glow of the setting sun, he creates something strange by simply insisting on certain forms of nature. *The Animals Sick with the Plague* reaches perfection in the genre: "this evil which spreads terror" is represented by a scene of epizootic disease in the middle of the desert, with the stricken beasts almost suffocating under miasmas.

Recent biographies of Gustave Moreau fix the number of watercolors on La Fontaine at 65, but this number refers only to the Antony Roux collection. There were in fact 83 if one is to believe Robert de Montesquiou who enumerates them and describes 57 of them. It is to be regretted that no edition of the Fables has been done with these illustrations, and that they have been dispersed and for the most part, lost. These watercolors are as complete as small-format paintings, and Ary Renan,

Illustration for a Fable
of La Fontaine:
"The Town Rat and the Country Rat."
Watercolor    28 x 21 cm.

Gustave Moreau Museum.

66

talking as a painter, was right to say, "There is no trace of fatigue, no study of calligraphy, of miniaturism; the rarest delicacies are washed in great strokes of water, and put down as light as a feather on the vellum, and the relative thick strokes, brushed over dry, play the role of fleshiness and add to the mystery of the background."

So we must accept this paradox: the best illustrator of La Fontaine's fables, the one who could best see what universal qualities they concealed, was Gustave Moreau. One only has to compare him with the other painters who approached this subject - for example Jean Baptiste Oudry whose drawings made up the 275 engravings in the 1760 edition, or J.-J. Granville with his animals disguised as humans - to see how much better he is than his predecessors; they attached themselves to the anecdotal and literally restricted themselves, whereas Moreau sets free the essence of the poetic statement. He exalts the power of the fable, which is less in its morality than in the enchantment that it brings to the mind by transporting it to a time when animals spoke. Thus he revealed the heart of his art, so much so that it is preferable to see these admirable illustrations, which are in fact recreations, before seeing the rest of Gustave Moreau's work.

Illustration for a Fable
of La Fontaine:
"The Oak and the Reed."
Watercolor    19 x 16 cm.

Gustave Moreau Museum.

# The master and his pupils

In 1892 Gustave Moreau became a teacher at the École des Beaux-Arts, and he took over the studio left empty by the death of his friend Élie Delaunay; he accepted this responsibility at the age of sixty-six in honor of his friendship with Delaunay, who was a sort of monk of painting and most original in character. The authorities ratified his nomination with joy, for they hoped that his prestige and his highly acclaimed ideal would outweigh the growing fashion of impressionism and put youth back on the path of tradition. It was also known that Moreau did not approve of the excesses of symbolism. Paul Leprieur tried to separate him from it: "The young literary school, led by M. Huysmans, has recently expressed an admiration for him which is sometimes compromising. It admires him blindly without understanding him: it would willingly raise an altar to him between Stéphane Mallarmé and Odilon Redon. But he must be distinguished from these wellknown deranged people."

Hercules and the Hydra.
Pen   21 x 16 cm.

Gustave Moreau Museum.

He went on to explain: "In fact his art is but an exalted and refined romanticism, made subtle in a way, which he applies to ancient subjects which are always loved by the Academies." One expected him to curb imagination with classical teaching, tempered with some romantic boldness. He conceived of his role quite differently and during the six years of his teaching, was the most stimulating and best loved teacher at the school.

As soon as he started Gustave Moreau devoted himself with passion to his mission as educator, not sparing any effort. Whereas the other teachers never spent more than twenty minutes in their respective studios where they pontificated, before going to show off in more worldly surroundings, Moreau would stay in his studio for more than two hours, taking an interest in each case, explaining his corrections with infinite patience. He was, however, under no illusion: *"If I leave behind two or three good painters, or even just one, I will be happy."* This result would be worth all his efforts. Georges Rouault said, "He arrived first at the School and was the last to leave. One could often find him in the Murier courtyard or in some corner sketching some antique in his little album. When he left the novices would hang on to his coat tails crying, "M. Moreau, correct us!" He was younger in spirit than many of us." Any beginner with a letter of introduction could go to his home; he would receive them with an exquisite and debonair courtesy, examine their drawings attentively, give them the necessary advice to put them on the right path. After one year Moreau's studio had the

Study.
Pen and pencil   17 x 18 cm.

Gustave Moreau Museum.

reputation of being the one where students worked the best, and his pupils were warmly congratulated at the annual, exhibition of works at the school, the jury deploring unanimously the fact that they could not do more to reward them.

The young Belgian painter Henri Evenepoel, who came from Brussels to go to Moreau's studio, wrote letters to his father describing the atmosphere. He recalls their first meeting when "his old servant, a tall skinny old maid," let him in and led him to the room where his host greeted him without ceremony and on looking at his work agreed to include him among his pupils. "The room we were in, his white beard, his smiling face, his small bright eyes, his childish look that took me in, standing by the lamp while the servant pulled the curtains, all this gave the impression of the artist living simply at home for his art." The old man holding the lamp led on the confused and stammering student. During the months that followed Evenepoel was full of admiration for the way that this teacher taught art just as Peter the Hermit preached the Crusade. Moreau warned his pupils against a technique with no soul: *"It is not enough to paint well; even among the masters of virtuosity the profession is not enough to maintain them at the level of those clumsy Byzantines who in a deformed and poorly composed head of a Virgin have elevated themselves to a feeling of ideal that has not been surpassed."* He told them that *"beautiful color"* depended on interior vision: *"one must copy nature with imagination, that is what makes one an artist. The color must be thought of, dreamed of, imagined..."* On another occasion Moreau said,

74

*"Enjoy thinking! Do not be afraid from time to time to sit down on your chair in the evening and let yourself think about everything beautiful and good that can be expressed in a thought, a thought that you have nurtured and loved with all your sensitivity."* Evenepoel was proud to have such a teacher who, whenever he had any doubts, received him without even removing his cap and his smock and treated him as an equal.

Gustave Moreau was venerated by his pupils like some secular saint. His modesty made him regret it and he would say to them, *"Do not respect me so much, love me a little."* He would have nothing to do with the cult devoted to him and everyone regretted that they could not obtain a photograph of him: "The photographers have no portrait of Moreau. No one at the studio knows of one. He has a horror of publicity," wrote Evenepoel. Moreau did everything to be a friend rather than a teacher. During his lessons he would give practical advice: *"Be careful of your eyes, always place the lamp behind you, do not work in fading light,"* etc. On Sundays he invited them to his home to look at the sketches they had done out of the School. When they were painted unconscientiously he would protest, *"My friend, you bring me daydreams!"* He often took them to the Louvre to look at Poussin and artists of the 15th century. Rouault tells us, "Long before Poussin became fashionable I made long visits to the Louvre with the good Gustave Moreau; then in the evening, often four days a week, we would have leisurely discussions just for the pleasure of exchanging impressions, not out of any desire to argue, for he erected no barrier between teacher and pupil, just a fundamental simplicity and a great desire to enlighten us." If necessary he did not hesitate to go to the homes of his pupils. When Matisse was bedridden with violent neuralgia, Moreau climbed up the stairs of his old house in St. Michel and stayed at his bedside for more than an hour; he took the opportunity of giving his opinion on the still lifes that Matisse was to send to the "Indépendants."

The members of the Institute who thought that Moreau would put youth under the academic rule were quickly to be disappointed; a muffled hostility was expressed for him. In fact he did not push his pupils to imitate him or anyone else; he encouraged them to express themselves frankly according to their own inspiration. He said, *"Send me packing if you think it right."* The only one who dared was Albert Marquet, who said to his neighbor after a session at the studio: "Come now, we are going to paint omnibuses." Moreau called him with a smile, *"my intimate enemy."* He was decried by his colleagues because he allowed his pupils to paint modern subjects, instead of confining them to historical painting. For the Beaux-Arts exhibition, when Evenepoel wanted to submit *The Cave of the Golden Sun,* he exclaimed: *"But you cannot show that, they will kill me!... Yet I really want you to!"*

Moreau visited all the exhibitions with indefatigable curiosity and pointed out paintings to his class that the official critics had ignored. He praised Toulouse-Lautrec from the beginning:

Landscape.
Charcoal    23 x 14 cm.

Gustave Moreau Museum.

*"Have you seen at an art dealer's on the rue Lafitte a woman sitting in a bar? She is painted in absinthe! You must go and see it."* He was the first to admire Rousseau at the "Indépendants": *"It is painted as though by a primitive and it appears that it is the work of a poor customs officer who only picks up his brushes during his days off."* Rouault added, "He went to the "Indépendants" at the heroic time. He would have gone to the other side of Paris if I had told him of an interesting work."

Moreau wanted to instil in that generation a contempt for facility. When a pupil left his studio to start his career, he made the following wish: *"I wish you late success and that you never come under any depressing influence."* His convictions were so noble, his words so burning that he fired all those young people with enthusiasm. Evenepoel said, "The things he told us were so beautiful, or seemed so beautiful to me, that it always made me want to cry; he positively provokes emotions!" And Rouault added with the same fervor, "Who can say what he meant to us apart from his work?... What he wanted to make blossom within us... those admirable conversations about the Masters, the constant concern about respecting our personalities?"

The number of pupils Gustave Moreau had in a short space of time was very high. The École des Beaux-Arts register shows 125, but there were also those who were not registered. All these pupils took different paths; the most famous were those who took part in the creation of fauvism:

The Roman Countryside.
Gouache    22 x 39 cm.

Gustave Moreau Museum.

Gustave Moreau, 58 Rome (Florence)

Henri Matisse, Albert Marquet, Henri Manguin, Charles Camoin. Among the others Georges Desvallières devoted himself to sacred art, René Piot to theatrical decor, Henri Evenepoel and Charles Milcendeau died too young to have given their best; Fernand Sabatte, Marcel-Béronneau painted *Chimerae* and *Salomés*. Less well remembered are Paul-Louis Baignières, Jules Flandrin, Charles Guérin, Simon Bussy, Léon Bonhomme. Henri Dabadie and Léon Lehmann each had is moment of brilliance. But although he tried to give everyone his equal attention, his favorite was Georges Rouault, in whom he saw the authentic inheritor of his pictorial doctrine. In his correspondence with André Suarès Rouault talks of the jealousy caused by the fact that he was a favorite disciple: "Gustave Moreau caused a lot of displeasure among his pupils by saying that I lived in perfect conditions of simplicity and isolation, and he added that that was how an artist worthy of the name should live." Exhibitions were held at various intervals, showing a selection of Gustave Moreau's works and those of his pupils thus giving truth to the assertion he made to them: *"I will be the bridge over which you will all pass."*

Study of the Sky.
Watercolor   47 x 29 cm.

Gustave Moreau Museum.

# A passionate silence

"Painting is a passionate silence," said Gustave Moreau. In the last years of his life he applied this precept to its ultimate consequence. But he remembered having said elsewhere about his paintings, *"If you like them, then you can hear their music, our music, we who above all must be painters."* He wanted to create the music of silence, compose grandiose operas like Richard Wagner, which are addressed to the sight, not to the hearing, symphonies that one listens to with one's eyes, at length, caught in a tumultuous eddy, feeling the magic power of sounds, smells, and colors intermingle. The watercolors of that period followed this evolution: they kept their rare and iridescent tones of stained glass or enamel, but they no longer had the precision of miniatures. The subject matter is no longer primordial, it is no longer a question of imposing it by illustrating it sumptuously; Moreau is more concerned with matching colors and transmitting states of mind. The finesse that he searches for is not

Villa Borghese.
Watercolor    28 x 44 cm.

Gustave Moreau Museum.

82

in order to saturate the atmosphere with luminous dust - what he called *"painting with the dust of the wings of a butterfly"* - but in order to enliven the lyrical feeling of certain themes.

The great paintings in which he followed his Wagnerian ambition were unfinished, so beyond human capabilities were these. Their execution demanded several lives. *The Chimerae,* that "satanic Decameron," started in 1884, symbolizing dreams born of the seven deadly sins, in a swarm of women agitated by ideas of lust, pride, or envy; *The Triumph of Alexander,* an impression of vast space, of inaccessibility, with the conqueror on a monumental throne in front of the people bringing him their tributes; *The Pretenders,* the bloody massacre by Ulysses of the young princes who sought after Penelope; *The Return of the Argonauts,* that "apotheosis of youth," and its cohort of figures grouped at the prow of the ship Argo: all these epics are even more moving by the fact that they are unfinished. In a less vast format *Jupiter and Semele* shows by its richness and the complexity of its colors, the intention of orchestrating painting, of making the colors sing. The drawings and watercolors that accompany the genesis of these paintings express above all the chromatic climate in which the desired forms must flourish.

The tendency to move toward the sacred increased with time in Gustave Moreau and ended in *Mystical Flower,* a majestic Virgin blossoming at the top of a giant plant. He had always had a grave sense of religion which led him to write in his diaries: *"Like a Chartreux I have busied my mind with ancient days and eternal things: such is my life."* But he was not a practicing believer:

Landscape.
Watercolor    16 x 23 cm.

Gustave Moreau Museum.

Gustave Moreau

his parents were agnostics and had given him no religious instruction; he was pantheist in his youth, and he invoked Apollo and Jupiter as though he believed in them. In 1874 he refused to decorate the chapel of the Virgin in the Panthéon on the pretext that he did not feel suited to frescoes. He painted an unusual *Adoration of the Magi,* in which the three magi represented the white, yellow, and black races. He did however sometimes deal with Christian subjects including crucifixions, angels, saints, but it is noticeable that he did so at times of suffering: thus after the death of his mother he undertook *Christ and the two thieves.* He reserved Christian themes for the expression of pain and resignation, believing that pagan themes suited him better when he wished to symbolize the forces of life.

He decided to make posterity the judge of his works by erecting a museum where people could contemplate the whole of his works. In 1895 he resigned himself to enlarging his paternal home: the ground floor was kept as it was, two floors were added and the façade was consequently altered. During the works which lasted more than a year, he took refuge in a flat nearby, the discomfort of which is described to us by Robert de Montesquiou: "I visited him once in this temporary home. He received me in a small bedroom all cluttered with furniture and paintings." At that time he made the following portrait of the painter: "He was irritable and sensitive, stubborn and obstinate in his opinions, intransigent in his judgments, fierce but kind, unapproachable but full of grace. If a contradiction or a different opinion were respectfully expressed he was quick to be angry, although his temper would just as quickly subside."

The Bosco at Rome.
Pastel   20 x 24 cm.

Gustave Moreau Museum.

Villa Borghèse_Académie de France.                    ~ Gustave Moreau ~ ROME ~ 18

When his age and decline in health got too much for him, one of his pupils, Henri Rupp, came to live with Gustave Moreau and devoted himself entirely to him, working as secretary and assistant, preparing his canvases, receiving his visitors. Moreau worked till he dropped, even when he was ill, putting to use even his feverish ideas. Coming out of a particularly bad crisis he said to Rupp, *"I have found a perfect costume for a Salome,"* and drew it with a shaky hand. For *The Pretenders,* not being strong enough to hold his palette he had the outlines drawn on the canvas according to his instructions which he would add to when he recovered. His last project was in 1897, a painting, *The Dead Lyres,* for which he only had time to do oil and watercolor sketches, and which opposed to the *"lyre of the pagan poet"* a cross held by an archangel, *"the cross, sublime symbol of sacrifice, of scorn for ephemeral things, supreme evidence of the adoration of the eternal divine."* He was not disallowing what he had painted previously, but exalting the final moment when *"the great lyre of the soul, the great voice of the really divine ideal extinguishes and abolishes all the voices of the senses which are glorified by nature."*

When he died on April 18, 1898, his pupils gathered together to watch over him and Georges Desvallières tells us, "Must we admit that even in front of his coffin, the clearest of our prayers was a long controversy about the role of thought in art? Day broke and the arguments supporting one thesis or another were going back and forth. Thus in front of the inanimate body of our master, his thought still animated us...." He had insisted on no one being invited to his funeral so that only those who wished to would come.  Degas was in the long cortège, and in order to justify the break in their relations, grumbled: "Moreau was the kind of man who starts by pulling back his feet so that no one can walk on them."

The inauguration of the Gustave Moreau museum took place at the end of 1902 after two years of discussions and alterations.  Unfashionable and nonconformist, this little temple of dreams became a center of attraction for people with refined taste.  Jean Lorrain in his novel *Monsieur de Phocas,* describes the intoxicating effect of a visit to the Gustave Moreau museum.  His hero is a neurotic who is searching everywhere for a supernatural color which obsesses him: "the glimmer of a jewel or a look, I am in love, worse, under a spell, possessed by a glaucous transparency; it is like a hunger in me.  I look in vain for this glimmer in eyes and in stones, but no human eye has it." In the end friends advise Phocas to visit the Gustave Moreau museum and there, lost and wandering among the paintings, he finds the impossible color in the eyes of the two adolescents in *The Pretenders.* "Those eyes were alive like two phosphorences, two calyxes of flowers."

Those who today visit the Gustave Moreau museum, or look through a book such as this one containing traces of his genius, realize what a salutary example he sets.  It is right that such a painter should appear from time to time, reminding us that contemplation is as worthy as action, that the silences of painting rival the eloquence of the sound of instruments and voices, and the purity of an artist's life makes for the greatness of art.

IMPRIMERIE-RELIURE MAISON MAME, TOURS.